Motivating Thoughts
Of
Kalam

Motivating Thoughts Of Kalam

PRASHANT GUPTA

Published by
PRABHAT PRAKASHAN PVT. LTD.
4/19 Asaf Ali Road,
New Delhi-110 002 (INDIA)
e-mail: prabhatbooks@gmail.com

ISBN 978-93-5521-422-5
MOTIVATING THOUGHTS OF KALAM
by Prashant Gupta

Edition
2026

Price
₹ 300 (Rupees Three Hundred Only)

Printed at
R-Tech Offset Printers, Delhi

Contents

A Brief Biography of Dr. A.P.J. Abdul Kalam

A source of inspiration for every Indian, the country's twelfth President, Abul Pakir Jainulabedin Abdul Kalam was born on October 15, 1931 in Rameshwaram in Tamil Nadu. His father, Jainulabedin, and mother, Aashiamma, were simple, religious-minded people and held an honourable place in society. They lived as a joint family.

Kalam's father never cared for luxuries and gave importance to rational thinking and human values. The senior-most priest of Rameshwaram Temple, Pandit Lakshman Shastri, was his dear friend. They used to have long spiritual discussions and Kalam, as a boy, listened attentively to those discussions and was deeply influenced by them in later life. Even as a child, Abdul Kalam was honest, God-fearing, and industrious with the simple traits he inherited from his parents. A simple man, his favourite meal remains garnished rice, *sambhar*, pickles and fresh coconut *chutney* served on a banana leaf like his mother used to prepare.

Dr. Kalam's childhood was deeply influenced by his cousin Shamsuddin who was the sole distributor of newspapers in Rameshwaram. During those days there was a great demand for *Dinamani*, a Tamil newspaper. Though Kalam had not yet learned to read he would take a keen interest in looking at the pictures.

In 1939, when the Second World War broke out, Kalam was only 8 years old. At the time, there was a sudden increase in the demand for tamarind seeds in the market. Seeing this, Kalam started collecting the seeds and selling them at the grocery shops in the town earning one anna every day.

During the war, an emergency was declared in India. As a result, the trains no longer halted at the Rameshwaram station and bundles of newspapers were thrown from the moving trains between the Rameshwaram and Dhanushkodi stations. Shamsuddin felt the need of an assistant who could help him to pick up those bundles. The little Abdul Kalam was ready to help him and was happy to earn his first salary from his cousin Shamsuddin.

When Kalam was in Class V in the local primary school, the new class teacher did not approve of Kalam, a Muslim, sitting in the front row with his Hindu friend, Ramanand Shastri. He ordered Kalam to sit on the last bench. The little boy did not like this; Ramanand Shastri too resented the teacher's arbitrary behaviour.

When Lakshman Shastri, Ramanand's father, heard about the incident, he sent for the teacher and reprimanded him saying, "You should not sow the seeds of religious discrimination in the hearts of innocent children."

The teacher apologised and, in time, his attitude changed completely.

Having completed his primary education, Kalam was admitted to Swartz High School in Ramanathapuram where he had to stay in the school hostel. Though he very often missed his parents and his home, he was dedicated to his studies and worked hard because his parents and teachers had high expectations from him.

Once, at school, it so happened that his maths teacher, Ramakrishna Aiyyar, was teaching another class. Unknowingly,

Kalam entered the classroom. The teacher immediately caught him by his neck and hit him with a rod before the entire class. Later, when Kalam secured the highest marks in mathematics, Ramakrishna Aiyyar narrated the episode during the morning assembly before everyone. He announced, "The boy whom I beat with a rod, will become a great man one day. Mark my words, this student is going to become the pride of his school and teachers."

Even in his childhood Kalam admired the mysteries of the sky, and the flight of birds across the seas. He enjoyed the sight of cranes flying over the sea and the long flight of birds. He decided then that one day he too would go for long flights in the sky. Eventually of course he was the first person in Rameshwaram to fly in a plane.

When Kalam completed his schooling, he was brimming with enthusiasm and confidence. He entered Saint Joseph College, Tiruchirapalli, in 1950. In college, as in school, he was an industrious and a disciplined student. In his final year at college he developed a fondness for English literature. He read all the books he could find of writers such as Tolstoy, Scott, Hardy, and other great European writers. He also found great pleasure in reading about astronomy, particularly our solar system.

To fulfil his dream, Kalam decided to study Engineering after completing his B.Sc. from Saint Joseph College. For this, he needed at least Rs. 1000, but his father did not have that much money. It was his elder sister, Johra, who came to his rescue. She mortgaged her gold bangles and necklace so Kalam could be admitted to the Madras Institute of Technology (MIT). At that time Kalam had planned to become a pilot.

At MIT, Kalam, because of his humility, was hesitant to ask questions, express his doubts or answer questions in the presence of everyone in the class. That is why his fellow students used to make fun of him. This depressed the young Kalam and made his lack of self-confidence even more acute. But then he would remember his father's teachings and inspirational advice. His father had often said: "One who understands others, learns; but a person is called wise when he understands himself. Learning without wisdom is nothing but crammed knowledge; it is of no use. Knowing oneself is more important." And this thought would restore his self-confidence and he would be recharged with enthusiasm to achieve his objectives. At MIT, Kalam was inspired by three teachers—Prof. Spander, Prof. K.A.B. Panadalaiin and Prof. Narsingha Rao—who gave his thoughts concrete form. Kalam was able to construct his work field with the joint assistance of these teachers who helped to lay the foundations of his life.

After completing his third year from the Madras Institute of Technology, he joined Hindustan Aeronautics Ltd. as a technical instructor. He soon reached the position of aeronautical engineer at Hindustan Aeronautics Ltd., and received two excellent job opportunities, both of which were enough to fulfil his childhood dreams. One was in the Indian Air Force and the other in the Technical Development and Production Directorate, Ministry of Defence. Kalam, with his well-preparedness, was certain he would be selected in the Indian Air Force.

But he was deeply disappointed when he discovered that out of 25 candidates, only 8 had been selected and he had stood ninth. It was a tremendous setback. But another chance still remained. Here he achieved success and was appointed Technical Assistant in the Technical Development and Production Directorate, Ministry of Defence, Government of India.

In the 1960s, Dr. Kalam joined the Vikram Sarabhai Space Centre, Thumba (Kerala) where he played a key role in the development of the first indigenous satellite launcher. In 1982, he took over as Director of the Defence Research and Development Organisation and was in charge of the Joint Controlled Launcher Development Programme. He then served as Scientific Advisor to the Defence Minister and later, as Defence Advisor to the Prime Minister. He also played a pivotal role in the success of the 1998 nuclear tests conducted by India. This success won him the title of 'The Missile Man'.

Dr. Kalam always paid attention to the ideas of his colleagues. He never attempted to impose his ideas upon them. He would maintain discipline and mutual understanding in his team and was friendly with all his colleagues. Because of these qualities, Kalam was a favourite among his colleagues. He was totally dedicated to his work throughout his life and work has been his companion. After retirement, Dr. Kalam taught at Annamalai University in Tamil Nadu.

While serving the country in various capacities, Dr. Kalam not only fulfilled the dreams of his parents and teachers but also his own. He put India on an equal footing with advanced countries and thereby enhanced its honour and pride.

Dr. Kalam received various prestigious awards. In 1981 he was awarded the 'Padma Bhushan'; in 1990, he received the 'Padma Vibhushan', and in 1997, he was honoured with the 'Bharat Ratna', the highest civilian award. Other than these, he was awarded the Dr. Virender Roy Space Award, the National Nehru Award and the Arya Bhatt Award. Twenty-eight universities throughout the country awarded him the title of Doctor of Science.

Dr. Kalam's achievements and the accolades are a result of his perseverance and strong determination. He had to face many obstacles throughout his life but nothing could deter him from the path. Whether it was an assignment as a scientist or as a teacher, he accomplished it sincerely.

Dr. Kalam was nominated President of India during his tenure as a teacher at Annamalai University. On July 25, 2002, he took the oath as the President of India by the then Chief Justice B.N. Kripal.

Dr. Kalam responded forcefully and sternly to the criticism of those who protested strongly against a scientist, 'The Missile Man', being appointed President. On July 25, 2007, he was succeeded by Mrs. Pratibha Devi Singh Patil.

Dr. Kalam gave a lot of attention to the students and youth of India. He regarded children as the seed in which the tree of the future is hidden. He not only had hopes from the younger generation, but also had full faith in them. His dream had always been an India where every child is educated. He believed we should nurture big dreams and the confidence in our hearts that will transform those dreams into reality.

Dr. Kalam believed that by 2020, our country can become a developed country, strong and self-reliant. This can turn into reality, not by the inspiration of a few select Indians, but by every Indian working together. The role of the younger generation is of utmost importance in the development of a nation. The youth is our most powerful resource, and his example is an inspiration for them to work together.

Dr. Kalam, besides being a capable scientist, an ideal teacher and an excellent writer, had a good knowledge of Indian classical music and played the violin too. He also loved gardening and, despite a very busy work schedule, he was regular with his morning walk, prayers and yoga. He believed we must keep ourselves busy every moment of the day in a meaningful way and, at the same time, take time off to enjoy the fragrance of blooming flowers or watch the myriad colours of the flitting butterflies.

As a visiting Professor to several Universities, Dr. Kalam evinced interest in visiting schools and interacting with young children. He continued this during his Presidency and has met 1 million children so far. Children in turn responded enthusiastically sending him thousands of letters and e-mails.

Recipient of India's highest civilian award Bharat Ratna, in 1997, Dr. Kalam was recognised as the face of 21st century India. He was also awarded the prestigious King Charles II medal for his contribution for promotion of science. He has also received an honorary doctorate from Carnegie Mellon University. He was the author of more than 15 books. Most of his books have been bestsellers for the past many years.

❑

A

Acceptance

I was willing to accept what I couldn't change.

Actions

- What actions are the most excellent? To gladden the heart of a human being, to feed the hungry, to help the afflicted, to lighten the sorrow of the sorrowful, to remove the wrongs of the injured!
- First, dreams transform into thoughts. Afterwards thoughts result into actions.

Agni Missile

Do not look at Agni
As an entity directed upward
To deter the ominous
Or exhibit your might.
It is fire
In the heart of an Indian
Do not even give it
The form of a missile.
As it clings to the burning pride of this nation
And thus is bright.

Agriculture

- Agriculture is the backbone of the nation. The nation cannot permit its development to wait.
- Agriculture needs a mission mode growth in development and production.
- Empowered agricultural service centres should be supported by a two-tier system through expert teams - at the district level and the national level.
- Converting agricultural waste as wealth, use of organic farming practices and also generation of bio-fuels from waste lands in the villages should be considered as a mission of the rural sector. The educational institutions, active DRDA and the Joint Director agriculture in association with NGOs should become facilitators for these programmes.

Aim

The young population of India must have an ambitious objective. A small aim is a crime.

Always think of rising higher. Let it be your only thought.

Amar Jawan Jyoti

"Lights our hearts with courage
Radiates to the nation, devotion
Spreads the message of sacrifice
Ignites confidence of our nation.
Triggers hope dancing in the wind
Scene of poise and serenity entwined

Upturned rifle and helmeted top
Altar of heroes, who fulfilled their promise.
Stately black granite and fire on all four corners
Deferential silence on their eloquent deeds
With floral tributes and moisture in our eyes
Amar Jawan Jyoti, we salute you in earnest."

Areas of Focus for Journalists

- Accuracy of news reporting
- Reporting real-time events in the rural environment, such as the weather report for fishermen or the right type of seed availability in the market
- Describing the life-pattern of farmers, fishermen, craftsmen and their seasonal needs, successes and problems
- Performance of panchayats and success stories, particularly of women panchayat leaders
- Progress and problems in the region—road condition, water-body condition and transport connectivity

Art

- Art helps to bring out the beauty of life in its noblest forms, imparting meaning and depth to human existence.
- Art helps life to survive.
- Art is a benign expression of the inner beauty in Nature. Be it a cartoon, sculpture or literary composition, it elevates the valiant spirit of life for everyone to see and enjoy.

Art of Happy Living

- Those who are responsible, simple, honest and diligent are personally honoured by God, for He says that they are His best creation on this earth.
- Help, at least, two poor girls for their education to make them self-reliant.
- Light a lamp in the life of someone.
- Have blessings, serve your parents, respect elders and teachers and love your country. Without them life is meaningless.
- Love all the creations of God.
- Giving is the highest and noblest virtue, but to complete it, it should be coupled with forgiveness.
- Divine beauty must enter into us.
- Every moment is a moment of creativity; don't waste it.
- Patience and tolerance is power; don't lose it.
- Learn from nature, where everything is hidden, and make your life purposeful and meaningful.
- These eyes are not going to retrace this world again; do your best.
- We must wear the gown of smile and our soul must wear the gown of virtues to protect it.
- Adopt simplicity and hard work, which is the only way to success.
- According to the Quran, there are seven heavens, but the eighth heaven has been created for those who do noble acts in the world.

- Keep and achieve the highest and noblest aims in your life.
- Be prepared for the questions that God would ask everyone: 'Could you become you?'
- Time, patience and Nature are the best physicians to remove all kinds of pains and heal all kinds of wounds.
- Patience is the power. Patience and time can transform even a leaf of the mulberry tree into silk.
- When God is with us no one can be against us.

Asset

The precious assets of a country are the skills, ingenuity and imagination of its people.

Authors

- It is the privilege of authors that they can help mankind endure adversities so they succeed in life.
- Authors act as conscience-keepers of the society.

❑

B

Beautiful hands

Beautiful hands are those that do
Work that is earnest, brave and true;
Moment by moment,
The long day through.

Believe in Ourselves

If we do not believe in ourselves and do not develop our technologies and work with them, the same thing will come to us from other countries with an alienated majesty. If we trust ourselves and rely on our own wisdom, technological dependence would be a thing of the past.

Book

- An inspiring book is a source of great knowledge and wealth for many generations.
- Coming into contact with a good book and possessing it is an everlasting enrichment of life.
- Five books in my life have been very close to my heart. I cherish reading them. They are—*Man the unknown*, *Thirukkural*, *Light from Many Lamps*, *the Holy Quran* and *The Bhagavad Gita.*

- Books are our eternal companions. Books gave me dreams. Dreams resulted in missions. Books helped me to undertake our missions confidently. Books gave mc courage at the time of failures. They were for me angels and touched my heart gently at the time.

Brain

The brain in itself is not intelligent. It is like a computer. You programme it and it will continue with its investigations. But at the end, the result of that search is always contained in the program, in the mind. So, it never discovers anything new. The best of brains are only supercomputers.

❑

C

Calamities

Have courage in combating calamities.

Candle

A candle loses nothing by lighting another candle.

Capacity Building

For building capacity, it is essential to increase the teacher-student ratio, improve the quality of teachers, provide them newer methods so that they upgrade their teaching skills, provide students with technology aids for becoming lifelong autonomous learners.

Change

Change is crucial. It brings about new thought; new thought leads to innovative action.

Child

- Ethical practices are taught by the father, mother and elementary school teacher. If the child is raised in this atmosphere, I am sure the child will maintain the righteous characteristics even when he/she encounters difficult circumstances.

- Once taught, children become conscience-keepers.
- Children are our greatest wealth and it is the responsibility of the State to allow every child to blossom. The first step that would enable us to fulfil this responsibility would be the identification of the child soon after his or her birth.

Citizenship

Enlightened citizenship has three components - education with value system, religion transforming into spiritual force, and creating economic prosperity through development.

Every citizen has a right to live with dignity; every citizen has a right to aspire for distinction.

Cleanliness

Always keep your home, your surroundings, neighbourhood and environment clean and tidy.

Common Man

In whatever field we work, we have to remain in the service of the common man whose well being is central to all human knowledge and endeavour.

Competitiveness

- Competitiveness has three dimensions—quality, cost and timeliness in the market.
- Competitiveness is the common factor between developed and developing countries.
- Competitiveness is the crown in the kingdom of sweat.

Computers and Gadgets

Most computers and gadgets of the future will be micro-sized, wearable and will have wireless communication with one another.

Conflict

Inner conflict is the very essence of violence.

Connectivity

Connectivity is strength; connectivity is wealth; connectivity is progress. Connectivity enriches societies.

Conscience

- Conscience is also a great ledger where our offences are booked and registered. It is a terrible witness. It threatens, promises, rewards and punishes, keeping everyone under its control. If conscience stings once, it is an admonition; if twice, it is a condemnation.
- Conscience is the light of the soul that burns within the chambers of our psychological heart. It is as real as life. It raises the voice in protest whenever anything is thought of or done contrary to righteousness.

Consciousness

Consciousness is not a construct. It is eternal. It continues. It is indeed a continuum. It is beyond the mind, which is, of course, beyond our brain.

Corruption

Corruption is an assault on conscience.

Country

Any country is as good as its citizens; their ethos, their values and their characters will be reflected in the country's make up.

Courage

Always be ready to think different;
Always have courage to invent,
Courage to travel onto an unexplored path;
Courage to combat problems,
And succeed in providing true information,
Are the unique qualities of the achiever.

Creativity

- Creativity is seeing the same thing as everybody else, but thinking of out-of-the-box solutions.
- Creativity is the foundation of human thinking and will always be at the highest end of the value chain.
- A beautiful ambience creates beautiful minds; beautiful minds lead to creativity.
- Creativity and imagination of the human mind would always be superior to any computer.
- I believe that the creativity of the human mind and the struggles it undergoes to achieve excellence can result in a person doing whatever he or she dreams of.

Cultures

Cultures are like many-hued glasses. Just as these glasses make colourless light to assume colour for them, cultures colour human essence.

Cyberspace

Cyberspace is the nerve centre of the station's critical infrastructure and is composed of hundreds of thousands of inter-connected computers, servers, routers, switches and fibre optic cables. It will add a fifth dimension to land, sea, air and space as a theatre for war and conflict.

❑

D

Death

Death has never frightened me. After all, everyone has to go one day.

Dedication

Be more dedicated in making solid achievements than in pursuing swift but synthetic happiness.

Desire

When you wish upon a star,
Makes no difference who you are;
Anything your heart desires,
Will come to you.

Determination

- If there is determination to achieve a goal, man will always succeed.
- With determined and concerted efforts, you can always succeed against established beliefs.
- We should not give up and we should not allow the problem to defeat us.
- Make every difficult task a possible venture.

Developed India

- To achieve the goals of developed India, a swift and bold national movement is essential. In this movement, every citizen, every constituent of our democracy has to participate. The citizen's participation can be in many important areas like reaching the unreached and to create awareness, feedback on service to the people, human resource development, entrepreneurship, home makers contributing to societal uplift, environment development, youth participation in the political system with the focus on developed India.
- The developed India will not be a nation of cities. It will be a network of prosperous villages empowered by tele-medicine, tele-education and e-commerce. The new India will emerge out of the combination of biotechnology, biosciences and agriculture sciences and industrial development.
- I will keep the lamp of knowledge burning to achieve the vision of developed India.
- An acceptable sign of a developed nation is the people 'who have' worked hard to bridge the divide between themselves and those 'who have not'.
- Encompassing the needs, rights and expectations of youth of the centre stage of development should be our priority.

Devotion

To succeed in your mission, you must have single-minded devotion to your goal.

Difficulties

Man needs his difficulties because they are necessary to enjoy success.

Dignity

The Courage of our conviction gives us strength and dignity.

Disability

Perception of disability lies in the mind.

Disaster

Overcome the impact of disaster through partnership.

Disgrace

It is not a disgrace not to reach the stars, but it is a disgrace to have no stars to reach for.

Districts

Clean panchayats lead to clean districts.

Doctors

When I see doctors I see them as pain removers.

As we light lamps, let us work and contribute in whichever way possible to reach help to those affected in recent mishaps and sufferings.

Dr. Ramanna

A towering and multifaceted personality, Dr. Ramanna was always keen to contribute to national development with a sense of mission in any capacity, which was evident in his role as a Union Minister and Member of Parliament.

Dream

- You have to dream before your dreams can come true.
- Great dreams of great dreamers are always fascinating.
- We must think and act like a nation of a billion people and not like that of a million people. Dream, dream, dream!
- Dreams transform into thoughts; thoughts result into actions.
- Dreams lead to the development of a nation.
- What I do know is that there is no greater power in heaven or on the earth than the commitment to a dream.
- Encourage all children to dream for themselves. Unless they have dreams, they will not be motivated to attain them.
- Dreams float on an impatient wind. A wind that wants to create a new order—an order of strength and thundering of fire.
- The dream-thought-action philosophy is what I would like to see inculcated in each and every student.
- Nurture a dream, let it live in your thoughts and kindle a fire in your belly.

Drinking Water

There are four ways to get safe drinking water: the first is to redistribute water-supply; the second is to save and reduce demand for water; the third is to recycle used water supplies and the fourth is to find new sources of fresh water.

❑

E

Economic Development

- A nation's economic development is powered by competitiveness.
- The competitiveness is powered by knowledge power.
- The knowledge power is powered by technology and innovation.
- The technology and innovation is powered by resource investment.
- The resource investment is powered by revenue and return on investment.
- The revenue is powered by volume and repeat sales through customer loyalty.
- The customer loyalty is powered by quality and value of products.
- Quality and value of products is powered by employee productivity and innovation.
- The employee productivity is powered by employee loyalty, employee satisfaction and working environment.

- The working environment is powered by management stewardship.
- Management stewardship is powered by creative leadership.

Education

- Education and values imparted in childhood are more important than the education received in college and university.
- A good educational model is the need of the hour to ensure that the students are developed as enlightened citizens and also participate in national development missions.
- There is a need for the inclusion of a 'moral science' class as a part of education in all the schools and colleges. This is essential for the promotion of value-based education leading to enlightened citizenship.
- Education with value system generates enlightened citizens.
- The mission of education is capacity building.
- Educational institutions should be equipped with adequate computing equipment, laboratory equipment, Internet facilities with high bandwidth connectivity and provide an environment for the students to enhance their learning ability.
- Educationists should build the capacities of the spirit of inquiry, creativity, entrepreneurial and moral leadership among students and become their role models.

- Our education system should re-align itself at the earliest to meet the needs of the present-day challenges and be fully geared to participate in societal transformation through innovation, which is the key to competitiveness.
- Real education is one that makes people think about or consider what they can do for the nation.

Empowerment

Only when each and every citizen has been empowered that he can lead a fulfilled life with dignity, will there be national peace and prosperity.

Energy

Energy-independence is India's first and highest priority. We are determined to achieve this by the year 2030 through three different sources, namely renewable energy (solar, wind and hydro power), electrical power from nuclear energy and bio-fuel for the transport sector.

English Language

English is necessary as, at present, original works of science are in English. I believe that in two decades' time original works of science will start appearing in our languages.

Entrepreneur

- Diversity of skills and perseverance in work makes an entrepreneur.
- The key characteristics required in an entrepreneur are desire, drive, discipline and determination.

Environment

A clean environment leads to a sound mind and body.

Equality

Each one of us on this planet creates a page in human history irrespective of who he or she is. I realise my experience is a small dot or microcosm in human history, but that dot has a life and light.

Experience

Experience stands between faith and falsehood.

❑

F

Fiscal Deficit

These changes will have a major impact on the fiscal deficit of states, apart from reducing the costs of doing business.

Flowers

Jumping deers, gliding ducks,
Smell of roses, daisy and lily;
Lotus and jasmine causing the soul,
Making the world a place to live;
To mould humans, as humans in deed.
See the flower,
How generously it doles out fragrance and honey.
It gives to all, gives freely its essence.
When its work is done, it falls away quietly.
Try to be like the flower, unassuming despite all its
qualities.

Footprints

If you want to have your footprints,
On the sands of time;
Don't drag your feet.

Foreign Goods

Why are we, as a nation, so obsessed with foreign things? Is it a legacy of our colonial years? We want foreign television sets. We want foreign shirts. We want foreign technology. Why this obsession with everything imported?

Freedom

If we are not free, no one will respect us.

Future

To live only for some unknown future is superficial.

Past meets the present and creates the future.

❑

G

Giving

O my fellow citizens,
In giving you receive happiness
In body and soul.
You have everything to give;
If you have knowledge, share it,
If you have resources, share them with the needy;
Use your mind and heart,
To remove the pain of suffering;
And cheer the sad hearts,
In giving, you receive happiness;
The Almighty will bless all your actions.

Globalisation

Globalisation is a shock to the indigenous industry. Stand up to it. Rise above it.

Goal

You must have a goal and dream enough; work hard and you will achieve what you want.

God

- God, our creator, has stored within our minds and personalities great potential, strength and ability. Prayer helps us tap and develop these powers.
- What has God promised: strength for the day; rest for the labour done, light for the way?
- Each individual creature on this wonderful planet is created by God to fulfil a particular role.

God's Message

You, the human race, is the best of my creation,
You will live and live;
You give and give till you are united,
In human happiness and pain;
My bliss will be born in you,
Love is continuum;
That is the mission of humanity,
You will see every day in the Life Tree;
You will continue to learn,
My best of creations.

- Removing the pain is God's mission.
- The work done to remove the pain is definitely God's work.

Goodness

I believe that goodness is a fundamental characteristic of essence. It is a timeless potential that might reveal itself at any point or any place. It is unblemished goodness, incorruptible goodness, indestructible goodness. It is not parcelled out to individuals. It is totally boundless, unlimited and endless.

Great heights

For people and a nation to rise to the highest, they must have a common memory of great heroes and exploits, of great adventures and triumphs in the past. All nations, which have risen to heights, have been characterised by a sense of mission.

Great Men

God loves those who are firm and steadfast. There have been individuals who bore patiently whatever befell them and continued on with their missions—whatever it was—faith, empire, mathematics, music and so on.

Great Minds

- The great minds radiate knowledge, which attracts young students to take difficult subjects and specialise with ease.
- The great minds of the country had the ability to make others join their endeavour to convert dreams into reality for them; the nation was bigger than them and they could draw thousands to act upon their dreams.

Great Souls

Enlightened souls bless the nation.

Greatness

Forgiveness gives greatness. Great leaders share the qualities of sacrifice and forgiveness.

Greatness of Flowers

Growing is our nature, destruction is theirs,
We are here to give the world
The message of God,
He takes us to decorate his palace;
He takes us to offer us to his God,
He takes us to garland his beloved;
Our touch makes him tender,
Our touch makes him humble.

Guiding Souls

Other than my parents and teachers, there are five persons, all of them scientists, who inspired and influenced me and whom I call the 'Guiding Souls'. They are—Prof. Vikram Sarabhai, Prof. Satish Dhawan, Prof. Brahm Prakash, Prof. M.G.K. Menon and Dr. Raja Ramanna.

❑

Happiness

In giving, you receive happiness.

Our service is your happiness.

Hard Work

All of us have to work hard and do everything possible to make our behaviour civilised in order to protect the rights of every individual.

Harmony

Harmony knows only the delight of the creator.

Human Beings

Human beings can attain lasting peace and happiness only when they rise above their selves and work towards serving others without external temptation.

Human Life

Poems are the result of peak happiness or sorrow. Common traits of both happiness and sorrow are tears. In one case, tears will be sweet. In another case, they will be salty. Human life is combination of both.

Human plight is the creation of minds.

I

I Am Great

I am an exquisite creation of God
God has blessed me to learn endlessly
With God's blessings, I will succeed and become a great human being

Ideals for Children

- You will study whole-heartedly.
- You will plant, at least, five trees.
- You will try your level best to remove the distress and pain of the downtrodden and the poor.
- You will make no discrimination on account of religion, caste and language.
- You will become honest and create a corruption-free society.
- You will celebrate the success of your country and compatriots.

Ideals for Media

- Media is a partner in development.

- Media has to be sensitive in reporting the progress and problems relating to rural areas. Media has to monitor and report progress periodically to asscss the efficacy of our system in reducing the people living below the poverty line, which is estimated to be 220 million.
- Media can propagate national successes particularly those emanating from rural areas, which will act as a great motivator and will also help spread the islands of successes to similarly placed regions in the country.

Ideas

Most sophisticated ideas start with a simple scribble.

Ignited Mind

Ignited minds of the young are the most powerful resource on the earth, above the earth and under the earth.

Ill-Effects of Addiction

Parents and teachers must constantly be with the children and tell them about the adverse or ill-effects of addiction. Also, the law-enforcing agencies must ensure that the peddlers do not hover around schools and colleges. In addition, parents should not pamper their children with an unlimited amount of pocket money.

Impossible

When people say something is impossible don't believe them. Nothing is impossible.

The word 'impossible' should be removed from the dictionary.

India

Clean states lead to clean and disease-free India.

Unless India stands up to the world, no one will respect us. In this world, fear has no place. Only strength respects strength.

India must achieve the real goal, that is energy independence or an economy, which will function well within total freedom from oil, gas or coal imports.

We will be remembered only if we give to our younger generation a prosperous and safe India resulting out of economic prosperity coupled with civilisational heritage.

India is a developing country. By 2020, it will be a developed country, meaning we will realise our goal: people below the poverty line to be near zero, literacy for all, quality employment opportunity for all, a very thin line between rural and urban areas leading to an economically prosperous, happy, safe and secure India.

India can design, develop and produce any type of missile and any type of nuclear weapon. This is a capability only four countries in the world have.

India is moving into the knowledge era. There is a need for transforming our society rapidly into a knowledge society.

We have to aspire to become the best in the world. We have a strength of 540 million youth who are below the age of twenty-five. We have to create 'I can do it' confidence in them. With that spirit, I am sure our youth will produce scientific discoveries and technological application, which will be world class.

In Memory of M.S. Subbulakshmi

You are the seven swaras of the instrument
Your music gave peace and lilt
You gave immense wealth along with music
You surprised God and made Him realise significance
of the human voice
Thousands and thousands of us were drenched by your
soulful music
Your mellifluous music moved our hearts and you were
a spring for 80 years
You were a star of women who wove garlands in
madhyamavati
You excelled in Sriragam and achieved great heights
in Bhakti sangeet to get Bharat Ratna
You made us realise the significance of Tansen's music
And you were a great gift of time
You excelled in the kirtanas of Annamacharya,
Purandaradasa and trinity of Carnatic music
By your voice you lifted the Tamil music
Even though you may have merged with time
Your music will live for a long time to come
Even though you have left this world for heaven
You lived in crores and crores of people here and will
Continue to live for music in the other world as well.

Information Technology

Information technology is a double-edged weapon. It provides vast opportunities but simultaneously introduces new vulnerabilities and threats, which may arise through computers, content and connectivity or, to express it differently, hardware, software, information and networks.

Innovation

It is through the process of innovation that knowledge is converted into wealth.

Innovation is capital.

Innovation is the key for non-linear growth.

Institutions

Institutions can create value, add wealth and develop great human resources.

Intention

When a person looks at himself, he is likely to misjudge what he finds. He sees only his intentions. Most people have good intentions and hence conclude that whatever they are doing is acceptable. It is difficult for an individual to objectively judge his actions, which may be, and often are, contradictory to his good intentions. Most people come to work with the intention of doing it. Many of them do their work in a manner they find convenient and leave for home in the evening with a sense of satisfaction. They do not evaluate their performance, only their intentions. It is assumed that because an individual has worked with the intention of finishing his work in time, if delays occurred, they were due to reasons beyond his control. He had no intention of causing the delay. But if his action or inaction caused that delay, was it not intentional?

Integrity

If you have integrity, nothing else matters. If you don't have integrity, nothing else matters.

❑

J

Jeevan Vidya

Jeeven Vidya is a 'teachable human value-based skill' that can address inherent conflicts within the mind of the individual, within families, in organisations and in public life. It develops tolerance for ambiguity and uncertainty in human conduct by enabling self-knowledge that understands harmony in the self and in the entire existence. The intelligent understanding of Jeevan Vidya itself can bring about a profound change in the consciousness of mankind.

Jeevan Vidya can lay the foundation of education in the young for evolving a conflict-free, happy life resulting in an attitude of 'giving'.

❑

K

Knowledge

- Knowledge without action is useless and irrelevant. Knowledge with action brings prosperity.
- Listening to everyone promotes knowledge.
- Man is the only creature engaged in the pursuit and advancement of knowledge on this planet, perhaps in the known universe.
- Blended knowledge is better knowledge.
- Knowledge revolution is indeed the foundation for leading India into a developed nation.
- The management of knowledge must move out of the realm of the individual and shift into the realm of the networked groups.
- I will keep the lamp of knowledge burning to achieve the vision of developed India.
- Learning gives creativity, creativity leads to thinking, thinking provides knowledge, knowledge makes you great.

- Thinking should become your capital asset, no matter whatever problems you come across or encounter in your life.

❑

L

Leader

- A leader sees far into the future.
- A leader gives the credit for success to those who worked for it and absorbs the failures.
- Quality leaders are like magnets; they attract the best people.
- The higher the proportion of creative leaders in a nation, the higher the potential of success of vision like 'Developed India'.
- When a leader empowers the people, other such leaders are created who can change the course of the nation itself.
- Leaders of my nation, please meet many people and help them, but you immediately look for those who need your utmost help and bring them to the mainstream.
- A productive leader must be very competent in staffing. He should continually introduce new blood into the organisation. He must be adept at dealing with problems and new concepts.

- Enlightened spiritual and scientific leaders all converge towards giving reverence to human life.

Leadership

- Creative leadership is exercising the task to change the traditional role from commander to coach, from manager to mentor, from director to delegator and from one who demands respect to one who facilitates self-respect.
- While moral leadership requires people to do the right things, entrepreneurial leadership requires people to acquire the habit of doing things right.
- Enlightened leadership is all about empowerment.

Assist other members who have similar disabilities by sharing knowledge and helping them to gather courage in order to overcome their problems due to disability.

An effective leader unites followers in a shared vision that will improve an organisation and the society at large. Good leadership must deliver 'true' value. This can happen only through integrity and trust. Thus, transformational leadership is different from a transactional leadership which builds power by doing whatever that results in more followers.

Ideal leadership defines a leader as one who moves his or her organisation forward in a positive direction. Given the right conditions, combined with adequate capital, the result is favourable not only to the particular organisation, but also to the society at large.

Legacy

We have a right and responsibility to leave a positive legacy to posterity for which we will all be remembered.

Life

- Life is a difficult game. You can win it only by retaining your birthright to be a person.
- There are forces in life working for you and against you. One must distinguish the beneficial forces from the malevolent ones and choose correctly between them.

Everyone's life is a page in human history irrespective of the position he or she holds or the work he or she performs.

The trouble is that we often merely analyse life instead of dealing with it. People dissect their failures for causes and effects, but seldom deal with them and gain experience to master them and thereby avoid their recurrence. This is my belief that through difficulties and problems God gives us the opportunity to grow. So when your hopes dreams and goals are dashed, search among the wreckage, you may find a golden opportunity hidden in the ruins.

Literature

Literature elevates and uplifts the mind.

❑

M

Manager

Leading and managing are two different ways of organising people. The manager uses a formal, rational method, while the leader uses passion and stirs emotions. A leader is someone whom people naturally follow by choice, whereas a manager must be obeyed. A manager may only have obtained his position of authority through time and loyalty given and not as a result of his leadership qualities. A leader may have no organisational skills, but his vision unites people.

Mankind

I believe it is our responsibility, the loving human beings of the planet earth, to look for an alternate habitat in other planets.

Medicine

Medicine is the most challenging field where human pain has to be combated with the best of human intelligence and care. Our mission is to give the confidence to smile.

Military

Radical change in military affairs has brought in new philosophies and concepts to warfare.

Mind

Brilliant minds are the source of creativity.

Every mind is creative; every mind is inquisitive.

An ignited mind is the most powerful resource on the earth, above the earth and under the earth.

The mind is an ocean. It contains so many worlds within itself, mysterious and dimly seen.

- A sound mind and body give rise to good thoughts.
- A great mind and a great heart go together.

Mission

What matters in this life, more than winning for ourselves, is helping others win.

The mission before the world today is to remove every tear from every eye.

Great missions are born out of great minds.

Mission of Human Life

Flowers blossom, radiate beauty and spread perfume,
And give honey;
On the eve of life,
Flowers silently fall to the earth they belong;
O my creation, this is the mission of human life,
You are born, live life of giving;
And bond the human life.
Your mission is the Life Tree;
My blessings to you my creation.

Mistakes

We must learn from our mistakes to achieve a better standard of life.

Music

Music is a great communicator and language can never be a barrier.

Music unites minds. It enters into the body and soul creating happiness.

Music penetrates into the soul and spreads happiness and kindness.

Music and Dance

- Music and dance elevate you to a different plane altogether and give you a breeze of happiness and peace.
- Music and dance can be used as an instrument for ensuring global peace and act as a binding force.

My Dear Soldiers

O defenders of our border
you are great sons of my land,
when we are all asleep
you still hold on to your deed.
Windy season or snowy days or
scorching sun, sweltering rays,
you are there guarding all the time awake.
Treading the lonely expanses as yogis,
Climbing the heights or striding the valleys
defending the desert or guarding the marshes

surveillance in seas and by securing the air,
prime of your youth given to the nation.
Wind chimes of my land vibrate your feet
we pray for you brave men
May the Lord bless you all.

My People

Remember all men are created equal,
The creator endowed them with inalienable rights;
Life, liberty and the pursuit of happiness,
Clue to the mystique of success;
Love for your work, faith in your dreams,
No force on earth can shatter your dreams.

Guide my people to develop an attitude to appreciate different ideologies and transform enmity among individuals, organisations and nations into friendliness and harmony. Embed the thought that a nation is bigger than an individual in the minds of the people's leaders. Oh God, bless my people, to work with perseverance to transform the country into a peaceful and prosperous nation.

Myself

What would you like to be remembered for? You have to evolve yourself and shape your life. You should write it on a page and that may be a very important page in the book of human history.

I am a child of God. I am greater than anything that can happen to me.

My mission in life is to bring connectivity between the billion hearts and minds of the people of India in our multi-cultural society, and to embed the self-confidence that 'we can do it'.

My mission is to protect our freedom from within, and from any external interference to make India politically, economically and socially a strong nation.

❑

N

Nanotechnology

Nanotechnology, which is the science of manipulating and characterising matter at atomic and molecular scales, and which integrates a multitude of science and engineering disciplines with widespread applications, warrants caution.

Application of nanotechnology is the development of smart materials. This term refers to any material designed and engineered at the nanometer scale to perform a specific task.

National

When the political leaders of a nation empower the people through visionary policies, the prosperity of a nation is assured. When religions are empowered to become a spiritual force, peace and happiness blossom in the society.

Nation

- All of us need to think and realise that the nation is greater than any one individual or organisation.
- A nation is great because of the way its people think.
- A Nation is on the path of prosperity.

- It is essential to ensure that the citizens are empowered with a decent quality of life encompassing nutritious food, comfortable habitat, clean environment, affordable healthcare, quality education and productive employment, integrated with our value system drawn from civilisational heritage leading to the comprehensive development of the nation that will bring smiles among one billion people.
- A nation fails not because of lack of economic progress but because of an increase in decision-makers with narrow minds.
- Nations are built over generations.
- A nation becomes superior in strength only by economic prosperity and defence capability.
- A nation consists of people. With their efforts a nation can accomplish all it could ever want.
- The needs of a nation's people are bigger and much more important than any other considerations.
- Capacity building is vital for national development.
- Integrated development is the key to national prosperity.
- National prosperity index is the reflection of inclusive growth.
- A nation is great, not because a few people are great, but because everyone in the nation is great. I visualise a Web of Life holding together and feeding the grass-roots of our Society with nutrients of our technological strength

and industrial prosperity.

- A nation is important compared to any individual, party or religion.
- It is the people of a nation who make it great. By their effort, the people in turn become important citizens of their great country. Ignited minds are the most powerful resource on earth, and the one billion minds of our nation are indeed a great power waiting to be tapped.

Nature

Nature is never in a hurry. It operates in terms of millions of years. A human life of 80 or 100 years is nothing but a tiny fraction in Nature's work. A human lifetime is just wasted if it is spent in an unawakened state or slumber.

Love nature and care for all its beings,

You will find God everywhere.

The basis of all systems—social or political—rests upon the goodness of men. No nation is great or good because parliament enacts this or that, but that its men are great and good.

Nurses

Nurses are teachers for the patients' families.

Nursing

Nursing is a dedicated mission.

❑

O

Optimism

My view is that at a younger age your optimism is more and you have more imagination. You have less bias.

❑

P

Patients

We need good hearts to treat the ailing hearts; we need helping hands to remove the pain and we need active minds to give happiness to patients.

Peace

For maintaining peace we have to be strong. All that we are doing is to create capability. Our policy is that of 'no first use'.

Peace in Space

The world's space community should avoid terrestrial geo-political conflict to be drawn into outer space, thus threatening the space assets belonging to all mankind.

Perseverance

One cannot stop at thinking and asking questions. There is need to act in order to solve our problems and that requires hard work and perseverance.

Hard work and perseverance are dutiful angels who will reside on your shoulders.

Philosophy of Life

The lamps are different,
But the light is the same.
Worldly joys you return to the world,
You remain in my innermost soul.

Poem For Physically Challenged Children

We are God's children
Our minds are stronger than diamonds
We will win, win with God's grace
When God is with us
Who can be against us?

Poverty

I will not get tired as long as the 260 million people below the poverty line in India do not smile.

Prayer to God

To God the Almighty,
Make my people sweat;
Let their toil create many more agnis that can annihilate evil,
Let my country prosper in peace;
Let my people live in harmony,
Let me go to dust as a proud citizen of India;
To rise again and rejoice in its glory.

- Create thoughts in the minds of my people,
And transform those thoughts into action.
Embedded in the minds of leaders and people

the thought of the nation being bigger than
the individual.

- Help all the leaders of my country with strength,
  And bless the nation with peace and prosperity.
  Give strength to all my religious leaders to bring
  Unity of minds among all our billion people.

- O Almighty, bless all my people to work and transform
  Our country from a developing into a developed nation.
  Let this second vision be born out of the sweat of my people,
  And bless our youth to live in developed India.

Pride

Defending the nation is our pride.

Problems

- Never let problems rule you.

- As the youth of our nation, you should not allow problems to become your master. You should become the master of the problems and succeed. If you take this approach, I am sure no impediment will be an obstruction for you.

- Problems present a challenge. Challenge propelled with knowledge and work leads to achievements.

- It is natural that we have to face problems and overcome them before achieving our ultimate aim in respect of any mission. We should have the courage of our conviction and strength of character to overcome the problem and succeed in our efforts. I have no doubt that we have both these qualities. God is with us.

Productivity

Partnership between scientists and farmers is a must for higher productivity and income. The most important action is to enable farmers to get quality seeds, quality fertilisers and quality pesticides from cooperative societies.

Progress

When learning is purposeful, creativity flourishes; when creativity blossoms, thinking emanates; when thinking emanates, knowledge is lit; when knowledge is lit, the nation progresses.

Shared vision is progress.

Let craft, ambition, spite be quenched in reason's right, till weakness turns to might, till what is dark be light, till what is wrong be right.

Prosperity

- Only positive thoughts lead to a prosperous and peaceful India.
- Connectivity and competencies lead to prosperity.
- Prosperity of nations is important for the prosperity of the world and to avoid conflicts and war. The centuries of learning from different civilisations should enable us to formulate ideas and systems to bring about prosperity and reduce disparities. One of the main drivers would be human values bridged by spirituality of religions.

PURA (Providing Urban Amenities in Rural Areas)

PURA envisages an integrated development plan with employment generation as the focus, driven by provision of the habitat, healthcare, education, skill development, physical and electronic connectivity and marketing in an integrated way for a cluster of villages with critical mass.

Purpose of Life

There is nothing in the entire universe that exists without a purpose. Purpose is central to a human life. The purpose of man's existence is not eating and sensual enjoyment.

Purposeless Activity

Endless, purposeless activity eventually leads to helpless feelings that perpetuate another cycle of more meaningless thoughts and actions.

❑

R

Reading

Give one hour a day exclusively for book reading and, in a few years, you will become a knowledge centre.

Real Teaching

A theoretical lesson coupled with a live practical example is real teaching.

Regional Prosperity

Convergence of core competencies is a must for regional prosperity.

Religion

No religion has mandated killing others as a requirement for its sustenance or promotion.

Remembrance

You will be remembered for creating a page in the history of the nation.

Repetition

Repeating what we did before for several decades with more of the same may not be the way to proceed further.

Research

Competent teaching emanates from research. The teachers' love for research and their experience in research are vital for the growth of any institution. Any institution is judged by the level and extent of the research work it accomplishes. This sets in a regenerative cycle of excellence. Experience of research leads to quality teaching and quality teaching imparted to the young in turn enriches research.

Righteous Life

- From the emperor down to the common man, the cultivation of righteous life is the foundation for everyone.
- Our righteous toil is our guiding light. If we work hard, we can all prosper. Nurture great thoughts; rise in actions. May righteous methods be our guide!
- If people who are in high and responsible positions go against righteousness, righteousness itself will get transformed into a destroyer.
- Righteousness is a conduct of eternal goodness and wholesomeness in human conduct - when we need peace in the world, we need order in the nation; we need harmony at home.
- When there is righteousness in the heart, there is beauty in character.

Role Model

It will not be presumptuous enough to say that my life can be a role model for anybody; but some poor children living in an obscure place in an underprivileged social setting may find some solace in the way my destiny has been shaped.

The nation requires role models in leadership who can inspire youngsters. There is no dearth of resources and talent in this country but what we need is more creativity.

❑

S

Sacrifice

Let us sacrifice our today so that our children can have a better tomorrow.

Satisfaction

Keep asking questions till you get satisfactory answers.

Science and Technology

Science and its pursuits are borderless.

The science that we work with today must have the innovativeness, foresight and the vision for it to be the centre of technology that we develop tomorrow.

Science is all about asking questions and finding the right answers through diligence and research into laws of nature.

- Science is a lifetime's mission.
- Scientific magnanimity is important for the growth of science. It will motivate the scientific community and nurture team spirit.
- Science is the foundation for societal transformation.
- Science is about converting challenges into opportunities.

- The pursuit of science is a combination of great elation and immense despair.
- Science and spiritualism seek the same divine blessings for doing good for people.
- The convergence of science and technology with spirituality is touted to be the future for both science, technology and spirituality.

I believe that there is nothing like bad science or good science. Science is indeed universal.

Scientists never claim absolute knowledge. Unlike a mathematical proof, a proven scientific theory is always open to revaluation, if new evidence is presented.

Sea Waves (Tsunami)

We are the children of sea waves,
Sea waves are my friends;
When they become angry,
Sea waves present challenges;
God has given the courage,
To challenge the sea waves;
And we will succeed,
We will succeed;
With Almighty's grace.

Self-Criticism

You must criticise yourself; you must consider everything that may contradict what you think, and you must never conceal an error.

Service

All God's creatures are his family; and he is the most beloved of God who tries to do most good to God's creatures.

Shadow

Between the conception and the creation, between the emotion and the response, falls the shadow.

Smile

My dream is to see a smile on everyone's face.

Society

- In a society, we have to build righteousness among all its constituents.
- The key characteristics required for a societal transformation and entrepreneurs are desire, drive, discipline and determination.

Song for the Jawan

Lights our hearts with courage
Radiates to the nation, devotion
Spreads the message of sacrifice
Ignites confidence of our nation

Triggers hope dancing in the wind
Scene of poise and serenity entwined
Upturned rifle and helmeted top
Altar of heroes, who fulfilled their promise

Stately black granite and fire on all four corners
Deferential silence on their eloquent deeds
With floral tributes and moisture in the eyes
Amar Jawan Jyoti, we salute you in earnest.

Song of India

"As a young citizen of India,
armed with technology, knowledge and love for my nation,
I realise, small aim is a crime.
I will work and sweat for a great vision,
the vision of transforming India into a developed nation,
powered by economic strength with value system.
I am one of the citizens of the billion;
Only the vision will ignite the billion souls.
It has entered into me;
The ignited soul compared to any resource
is the most powerful resource
on the earth, above the earth and under the earth.
I will keep the lamp of knowledge burning
to achieve the vision—Developed India

Soul

The soul is the locus, the agent, and all the varied content of human experience.

Space

- In space exploration may lie the solution to many earthly problems.
- I foresee that an important contribution for the future of space exploration by India would be space missions to the Moon and the planet Mars founded on space industrialisation.

- What better vision can there be for the future of space exploration than participating in a global mission for perennial supply of renewable energy from space?
- The space programme has touching the lives of many among the billion people of India in several ways.
- Space research is a technology-generator. It is truly inter-disciplinary and has enabled true innovations at the intersection of multiple areas of science and engineering. It is almost a 'Green Technology'. Its greatest asset is that it enhances the quality of human life on earth. Besides direct contributions, the fruits of space research have also resulted in designing innovative products such as cardiac stent and heart pacemaker for healthcare.
- Space research has had as its major focus on making things work and bringing the dreams of mankind to fruition through technologies that mankind can be proud of.
- Space technology can also be used for forecasting and modelling of volcanic eruptions, landslides, avalanches, flash floods, storm surges, hurricanes and tornadoes.

Space Vision 2050

World Space Vision includes five areas, which are important for the future of space science, technology and application. They are — interplanetary exploration and space industrialisation, low cost access to space and large scale societal missions, space satellite service station, necessity for keeping peace in space, management structure in international collaboration.

World Space Vision 2050 would enhance the quality of human life, inspire the spirit of space exploration, expand the horizons of knowledge and ensure space security for all the nations of the world.

Spirit

When you want to become a great corporate, you need indomitable spirit. the characteristic of indomitable spirit is that there must be a vision leading to higher goals.

States

Clean districts lead to clean states and clean states to a clean country.

Strength

Strength respects strength.

Climbing to the top demands strength, whether it is to the top of Mount Everest or to the top of your career.

Students

- Always realise that you have to set a goal in your life. To achieve the goal, you will acquire the knowledge, you will work hard, and when the problem occurs, you have to solve the problem and succeed.
- As a youth of your nation, you will work with courage to achieve success in all your tasks and enjoy the success of others.
- You will always keep yourself, your home, your surroundings, neighbourhood and environment clean and tidy.

- You realise that righteousness in the heart leads to beauty in the character; beauty in the character brings harmony at home; harmony at home leads to order in the nation and order in the nation leads to peace in the world.
- You will lead an honest life free from all corruption and will set an example for others including your home to adopt a righteous way of life.
- You will light the lamp of knowledge in the nation and ensure that it remains lit for ever.
- You realise, whatever work you do, if you do your best, you are contributing towards realising the vision of developed India 2020.
- The primary focus of students should be to excel in their studies. this is their first contribution to the development of the nation. The education system should instil in the minds of students capacities of inquiry, creativity, technology, entrepreneurial and moral leadership. If we develop in all our students these five capacities, we will produce 'Autonomous Learners', self-directed self-controlled, lifelong learners, who will have the capacity to both respect authority and at the same time be capable of questioning authority, in an appropriate manner. These are the leaders who would work together as a 'Self-Organising Network' and transform India into a developed nation in a time-bound manner.
- We must give our students the skills with which they find a way through the sea of knowledge that we have created

and continue with lifelong learning. We are empowered by technology to teach ourselves beyond classrooms and become lifelong learners. This is indeed required for sustained economic development of the nation and also individual prosperity.

- The hardest teaching is received and the toughest examinations are faced not in schools but, in the later years, out of schools.
- Be an exemplary student. Whatever do be the best. Then you are a patriot.

Success

- For success in all missions, we need creative leaders.
- If there is a solemn aim in one's life, irrespective of the hindrances and obstructions, the glow of the goal and our perseverance will nurture our goals, all through the surrounding difficulties, leading to success.
- Success always follows dreams attempted though there may be some setbacks and delays.
- Breathe success. I want youngsters to dream, aim high and work for the country's transformation.
- Success is powered by mission in life. Mission in life is powered by three great actions. Three great actions are acquisition of knowledge, hard work and perseverance. Knowledge is powered by great teachers and inspiring books. Hard work is powered by building daily habits. Perseverance is powered by will power.

Suffering

Suffering is the essence of success.

Sustainable development

- Political leadership the world over is incapable of rising to the challenge of sustainability.
- If higher education is the nursery of tomorrow's leaders then the sector bears profound responsibilities to create a sustainable future.
- Graduates of every discipline need a sound working knowledge about sustainability.

Sweat

Our sweat and commitment will transform developing India into a developed India.

❑

T

Team

Team creates environment; environment motivates the team.

Technology

Technology is the non-linear tool available to humanity which can effect fundamental changes in the ground rules of economic competitiveness.

The right signal is that technology is going to boost the economic development of our nation.

Technology's outreach is vital for rural transformation.

Today technology is the main driver of economic development at the national level. Therefore, we have to develop indigenous technologies to enhance our competitive edge and to generate national wealth in all segments of economy. Therefore, the need of the hour is to arm India with technology.

Terrorism

In our rapidly globalising world, threats and challenges such as terrorism, fundamentalism and extremism must be neutralised effectively through universal commitment and cooperation. we stand firm in condemning all forms and manifestations of terrorism.

Terrorism constitutes one of the gravest threats to global peace and security and violates the most basic human right—the right to life. The scourge of terrorism transcends international boundaries and needs to be countered by nations acting in close cooperation.

We in India are determined to fight it. Terrorism has the potential to damage economies and the social harmony of open societies like ours.

Think Big

The water in your jug,
Is brackish and low.
Smash the jug,
And come to the sea.

Thinking

Thinking is progress; non-thinking is destruction. Thinking leads to action.

- Thinking should become your capital asset, no matter whatever trials and tribulations you come across in your life.
- Thinking is progress. Non-thinking is stagnation of the individual, organisation and of the country. Thinking leads to action.
- Thinking is the basis for all inventions, which have led to progress.

Thoughts

What was considered impossible has happened and what is thought possible has not yet happened but it certainly will happen.

Away! Fond thoughts and vex my soul no more! Work claimed my wakeful nights; my busy days although brought memories of Rameshwaram shore yet haunt my dreaming gaze!

Thoughts do not come from outside; neither do feelings or images. They come from the soul and return to the soul, always within the soul.

Our thoughts are, most assuredly, things. They are conceived in the mind and travel through time and space like ripples in a pond affecting all that they touch. Thoughts are the building blocks of our experience. The world we see is the one we have created with our thoughts.

Three Pillars of Life

The three key societal members who can make a difference are father, mother and teacher.

Time

The time is always right to do what is right.

Tomorrow

Let us sacrifice our today so that our children can have a better tomorrow.

Training

Training is an important educational mechanism to remove life's disabilities.

Transformation

Transformation is an outcome of a farsighted vision, innovative mind and guiding spirit.

Tribute to M.S. Subbulakshmi

Your music with beautiful deeds,
Will live for a long time to come;
You were born in music, lived with music,
And now forever you are merged with divine music.

True Spirit

It has been my personal experience that the true flavour, the real fun and the continuous excitement of work lies in the process of doing it rather than in having it over and done with. The four basic factors that I am convinced are involved in successful missions: goal setting, positive thinking, visualising and believing.

Truthfulness

When you speak, speak the truth; perform when you promise; discharge your trust. Withhold your hands from striking and from taking what is unlawful and bad.

Twenty-First Century

The twenty-first century is about the management of all the knowledge and information we have generated and the value addition that we can bring to it.

❑

U

Universe

Look at the sky. We are not alone. The whole universe is friendly to us and conspires only to give the best to those who dream and work.

❑

V

Value System

Economic prosperity has to be complemented with the value systems and our five thousand-year-old civilisational heritage, which has genetically shaped the Indian people. When the nation is progressing towards economic development, it is also essential to build education with the value system drawn from our civilisational heritage. The good human life comes out of the way we live; we may have a series of problems but the billion people have the connectivity which gives us the united strength.

Villages

Clean and green villages lead to developed villages. Developed villages lead to developed India.

All 6,00,000 villages of India should be empowered to deal with their development and be well connected among themselves and with the urban societies.

The strength and wealth of India lives in villages.

If you don't do anything, there will be no problem. If you do anything, there will be a problem. And, the idea is to overcome and solve the problem instead of allowing it to master you.

The essential needs of the villages today are water, power, roads, sanitation, healthcare, education and employment generation.

Virtuous Man

A virtuous man alone can use the instrument of conscience.

Vision 2020

We have a population of one billion people, out of which 540 million people are below the age of 25 years. This national strength can transform us into a developed country. In addition, we have natural resources. Also, we have a road map for transforming India into a developed nation by 2020: Integrated action in the five areas of agriculture and agro-processing, education and healthcare, infrastructure, strategic systems and critical technologies. The ignited minds of the 540 million youth will definitely transform India into a developed country by 2020.

Vision

We should all create a nation that is one of the best places to live in on this earth and which brings smiles to a billion faces.

We have a vision of transforming India into a developed nation before 2020, energising and igniting the minds of all Indians. Scientists and technologists have an important role in realising the mission of developed India. To realise this mission, we need excellent minds for basic science, research, teaching and converting the results of research into applications for national development. Mutually beneficial international cooperation will be an important element of this transformation.

Vision ignites the minds. India needs visionaries of the stature of J.R.D. Tata, Vikram Sarabhai, Satish Dhawan and Dr. Verghese Kurien, to name a few, who can involve an entire generation in mission-driven programmes, which benefit the country as a whole.

You can achieve success only if you have vision, which translates into dreams, percolates into thoughts and turns itself into actions.

For the next 50 years we have three challenges. First, to eradicate poverty, second, to bring material from the Moon and finally, to set up a habitat in Mars.

Vision for the Nation

Nations are built by the imagination and untiring enthusiastic efforts of generations. One generation transfers the fruits of its toil to another, which then takes forward the mission. As the coming generation also has its dreams and aspirations for the nation's future, it, therefore, adds something from its side to the national vision, which the next generation strives hard to achieve. This practice continues and the nation climbs steps of glory and gains higher strength. Any organisation, society or even a nation without a vision is like a ship cruising on the high seas without any aim or direction.

Visionary

Mistakes can delay or prevent the proper achievement of the objectives of individuals and organisations, but a visionary can use errors as opportunities to promote innovation and the development of new ideas.

A visionary can build a new nation.

Visually Impaired

Making the lives of the visually impaired productive would be a tremendous contribution towards human resources.

❑

W

Way of Life

We have not invaded anyone. We have not conquered anyone. We have not grabbed or seized their land, their culture, their history and tried to enforce our way of life on them.

Well-Wisher

Always celebrate the success of your colleagues and friends.

While Looking Down from an Aircraft

My worthiness is all my doubt—
His merit—all my fear—
Contrasting which quality
Does however—appear.

Will Power

I learnt from failures and hardened myself with courage to face them.

Women

Women are equal partners in national development. When women are empowered, a society with stability is assured.

Womanhood is a beautiful creation of God. I am always inspired and rejuvenated by the memory of two great women, one, my mother and the other, Bharat Ratna M.S. Subbulakshmi.

Work

Good work is appreciated everywhere.

Worry

Don't worry and fret, faint-hearted, the chances have just begun. For the best jobs have not been started, the best work has not been done.

❑

Y

Year 2020

- A nation where the rural and urban divide has reduced to a thin line by establishing 7,000 rural clusters and providing urban facilities in them.
- A nation where there is an equitable distribution and adequate access to energy and quality water.
- A nation where agriculture, industry and the service sector work together in symphony.
- A nation where education with value system is not denied to any meritorious candidate because of societal or economic discrimination.
- A nation which is the best destination for the most talented scholars, scientists and investors.
- A nation where the best healthcare is available to everyone.
- A nation where the governance is responsive, transparent and corruption-free.
- A nation where poverty has been totally eradicated, illiteracy removed and crimes against women and children are absent and none in the society feels alienated.

- A nation that is prosperous, healthy, secure, peaceful and happy and continues with a sustainable growth path.
- A nation that is one of the best places to live in and is proud of its leadership.

Young Children

I want to reassure young children that all the pain that they inevitably go through in life is to allow them to evolve into accomplished individuals; develop a deeper understanding of who they are and where they belong to.

Youth

- A combination of knowledge, enthusiasm and diligence of the youth is the great dynamic fire for transforming the nation.
- I personally feel the young have the most powerful minds. They can overcome the negativity of the bureaucracy and some self-centred policies of the state governments and enrich the people of the country. They can even improve coordination between the states and the centre. And they surely will.
- Each and every Indian can make a difference, especially the nation's youth.
- Children and youth are the picture of a nation's future. They are our hope for tomorrow.
- If India is to become developed by 2020, it will do so only by riding on the shoulders of the young.
- The aspiration of the youth is to accelerate development and make India developed before the year 2020.

- Youth movement is a must for Developed India 2020. We have to empower the youth through value-based education and leadership.
- We have a roadmap for becoming an economically developed nation for fulfilling the aspirations of a billion democratic people of multi-religions, multi-languages and multi-cultures. Our human resources, particularly the 540 million youth, will make this mission a reality using science and technology as a tool with the available bio-diversity and natural resources.
- The youth irrespective of which country they belong to, aspire to live in a peaceful, happy, prosperous and safe nation.
- At present, India has 540 million youth under the age of 25 which will continuously grow till the year 2050. In the coming decades, India needs a large number of talented youth with higher education for the task of knowledge acquisition, knowledge imparting, knowledge creation and knowledge sharing.
- The youth have to nurture scientific temper. They have to look at issues with the right balance of rational thinking, logical approach and humanism.

Youth of the Country

Our youth should have a dream and work for transforming India into a developed nation. The youth can contribute to this mission by fixing a goal in their lives, combating hurdles, and achieving excellence. Students must imbibe moral values. They should aspire to become entrepreneurs. During holidays and their vacations, they can teach those who cannot read and write and underprivileged children. They can plant trees and improve the ecological balance.

❑

Various Oaths Administered by Dr. Kalam

Oath for Citizens of India

- Children are our invaluable wealth.
- For the development of our nation, we shall provide the same education to every boy and every girl without any discrimination.
- We should not squander or waste our hard-earned money in gambling and drinking.
- We should have small families for health and prosperity.
- We should teach our children the importance of education. Education leads to knowledge and knowledge makes children succeed in their mission.
- We should aim to protect forests and get rid of pollution.
- We should be role-models for our children.
- We should plant at least five trees in our houses or in our surroundings and nurture those with rain water stored through water harvesting.

- We should work for the development and prosperity of India.
- From now onwards we should teach, at least, those five persons who cannot read and write.
- Water is our asset. We will conserve every drop of water. We will activate at least one water pond in our villages or in our localities in partnership with village citizens.
- Tourists are our guests. We will provide all help to the tourists to make their stay in the state pleasant and purposeful.
- We will lead a righteous life derived from Indian heritage and culture and be a role model for our children.

Oath for Gram Panchayat

- Give importance to cleanliness to make the gram panchayat clean and pollution-free.
- Arrange for safe and clean drinking water for your villagers.
- Provide modern infrastructural facilities to every gram panchayat to make it prosperous and self-reliant.
- Try your level best to make every villager literate. Also, persuade every boy and girl to go to school every day.
- Rid the villages of the menace of water pollution. Dirty contaminated water should be discharged in an efficient manner.

- Carry out our duty with absolute transparency and honesty to make every gram panchayat self-dependent.
- Make every gram panchayat free from crime. Quarrels among several gram panchayats should be sorted out in a befitting manner.

Oath for Medical Professionals

- We, the medical professionals, realise that we are on God's mission.
- We will always give part of our time for treating patients who can't afford hospitalsation.
- We will treat, at least, 20 rural patients in a year at minimum cost by going to rural areas.
- We will encourage the development of quality indigenous equipment and make use of them in enhancing the quality and reliability of the products to be manufactured.
- We will follow the motto 'let my brain remove the pain of suffering humanity and bring smiles'.

Oath for Teachers

- First and foremost, I will love teaching. Teaching will be my soul.
- I realise that I am responsible for shaping not just students but ignited youths who are the most powerful resource

under the earth, on the earth and above the earth. I will be fully committed for the great mission of teaching.

- I will consider myself to be a dedicated teacher only when I can lift the average student to the best performance by way of my special teaching.
- I will organise and conduct my life in such a way that my life itself is a message for my students.
- I will encourage my students and children to ask questions and develop the spirit of enquiry so that they become creative enlightened citizens.
- I will treat all the students equally and will not support any differentiation on account of religion, community or language.
- I will continuously build the capacities in teaching so that I can impart quality education to my students.
- I will always celebrate the success of my students.
- I realise by being a teacher I am making an important contribution to all the national development initiatives.
- I will constantly endeavour to fill my mind with great thoughts and spread the nobility in thinking and action.

Oath for Jawans

- I am proud to belong to the Indian army of great tradition.
- I will always aim at winning, lead to victory of my nation.

- I will always be a useful citizen and be helpful to my countrymen when they are in distress.
- I will proudly celebrate the success of my country and my people.
- My flag is my life.

Oath for IAS Trainees

- Wherever I am posted I will work for hundred per cent adult literacy among the villagers, particularly the women and special children and also ensure that no child drops out from school.
- Wherever I am posted I will ensure that the status of women is enriched and work towards creation of parity between male and female births in the village.
- I will ensure that no one can lead me to the temptation of corruption.
- During my tenure in the district, I will ensure that at least one lakh trees are planted and maintained.
- I will work towards the execution of at least five PURA (Providing Urban Amenities in Rural Areas) complexes in the district and create employment opportunities for at least twenty-five per cent of the youth through creation of rural enterprises by local entrepreneurs.

Oath for Service to the Nation

- We will endeavour to transform India into a developed nation.
- We will help our compatriots to become disciplined citizens by being a role model.
- We will create a movement of making our own homes righteous, environment clean and excel in studies and in our tasks.
- We will fight against all the social evils including injustice towards women in our society and will provide a respectable place for our women in society.
- We will remove corruption from our society through knowledge and high moral values.
- We will strengthen the nation through national integration, national security and patriotism.
- We will inspire people to be law abiding citizens.
- We will prevent deforestation and protect the environment through planting of new trees.

Oath for Enlightened Citizenship

- I will love whatever profession I take up and will try to excel in it.
- From now onwards, I will teach at least 10 people to read and write who cannot read and write.

- I will plant ten saplings/trees and ensure their growth.
- I will go to rural and urban areas to reform at least five persons from the habits of addiction and gambling.
- I will take responsibility for removing the pain of ailing individuals.
- I will participate in the mission of realising the economic strength of India by combining it with an education with value system and by transforming religion into a spiritual force.
- I will not support any differentiation on account of community or language.
- I will lead an honest life free from all corruption and will set an example for others to adopt a transparent way of life.
- I will always be a friend of the mentally and physically challenged and will work hard to make them feel normal.
- I will celebrate the success of my country and my people.

Oath for People with Special Abilities

- I will not allow my special abilities to come in the way of my progress.
- I will work hard, and when the problem occurs, I will attempt to solve the problem and succeed.
- I will try to excel in every field by acquiring knowledge.

- I will assist other members who have similar disabilities by sharing knowledge and helping them to gather courage to overcome their problems owing to disability.
- I shall always keep my home, my surroundings, neighbourhood and environment clean and tidy.
- I will always celebrate the success of my colleagues and friends.
- We are all God's children, our minds are stronger than diamonds. We will win successfully with our mighty will. When God is with us, who can be against?

Oath for Youth

I will pursue my education or work with dedication and I will excel in it.

From now onwards, I will teach at least 10 persons to read and write.

I will plant at least 10 saplings and shall ensure their growth.

I will visit rural and urban areas and wean away at least five persons from addiction and gambling.

I will constantly endeavour to remove the pain of my suffering brethren.

I will not support any religious, caste or language differentiation.

I will be honest and endeavour to make a corruption-free society.

I will work towards becoming an enlightened citizen and make my family righteous.

I will always be a friend of the mentally and physically challenged and will make them feel normal.

I will proudly celebrate the success of my country and my people.

Oath for Courage

Courage to defend the nation, courage to innovate, courage to invent and courage to overcome the sufferings and to succeed, are indeed the traits that led to the growth of human civilisation. I, as a citizen of India, will work with courage and knowledge to transform my nation into a prosperous, happy and safe India.

Oath for Students

- I will pursue my education with dedication and will excel.
- I will teach at least 10 persons to read and write who at present cannot do so.
- I will plant at least 10 saplings and shall ensure their growth through constant care.
- I will visit rural and urban areas and permanently wean away at least 5 persons from addiction and gambling.
- I will constantly endeavour to remove the pain of my suffering brethren.

- I will not support any communal or language differentiation.
- I will work for becoming an enlightened citizen.
- I will always be a friend of the mentally and physically challenged and will work hard to make them feel normal, like the rest of us.
- I will proudly celebrate the success of my country and my people.

Unity in Diversity—People have equal respect and tolerance for all faiths. Hate and anger is substituted by love and peace. Religion graduates into spirituality. Universal brotherhood is followed by all citizens.

Is all this a dream? Dreams always become the vision, vision transforms into missions and missions generate hundreds of goal-oriented projects.

Oath for NCC Cadets

- National progress and development should be our aim.
- We will endeavour to transform India into a knowledge society.
- We will help our countrymen to become disciplined citizens by being a role model.
- We will create a movement of making our own homes righteous, environment clean and excel in studies and in our tasks.

- We will fight against all the social evils including injustice towards women in our society and will provide a respectable place for our women in our society.
- We will remove corruption from society through knowledge and high moral values.
- We will strengthen our nation through national integration, national security and patriotism.
- We will stop deforestation and plant new trees to protect our environment.
- We will work towards transformation of girl children and will provide them equal rights in society.

Oath for the Police Personnel

- I am proud of being the member of a Police Force of high tradition.
- I will always be citizen—friendly and promote peace everywhere.
- I will be lightning and thunder to all the law breakers.
- I will protect the elderly, women and children against any type of crime.
- I will be a role model for conduct and discipline.
- I will lead an honest life free from all corruption and set an example for others to follow.
- My nation is my life.

The National Prayer

The grand scene of birth of independent India,
In that midnight, the flag of the ruler of two centuries lowered,
The tri-color Indian flag flaps in the Red Fort in the midst of the national anthem.
The first vision of Independent India had dawned.
The people rejoice everywhere, happiness all around,
There was a tender cry: 'Where is the father of the nation?'
The white clothed soul walking in the midst of sorrows and pain,
Injected by hatred and ego, the result of communal violence.
The father of the nation, Mahatma, walking barefooted
In the streets of Bengal for peace and harmony.
With the strength of blessed soul of Mahatma
I pray to the Almighty: When will be the dawn of the second vision?
Create thoughts in the minds of my people,
And transform those thoughts into the nation being bigger than
The individual, in the minds of leaders and people.
Help all the leaders of my country to have strength
And bless the nation with peace and prosperity.
Give strength to all my religious leaders to bring
'Unity of Minds' among all our billion people.

Oh! Almighty, bless all my people to work and transform
Our country from a developing into a developed nation.
Let this second vision be born out of the sweat and dedication of my people,
And bless our youth to live in developed India."

❑

References

Books

1. 2020 : A Vision for the New Millennium
2. Children Ask Kalam
3. Day by Day Historical Study Vol. 1
4. Day by Day Historical Study Vol. 2
5. Envisioning an Empowered Nation
6. Family and Nation
7. Guiding Souls
8. Ignited Minds
9. Indomitable Spirit
10. Inspiring Thoughts
11. Mission India
12. My Journey
13. The Life Tree
14. The Luminous Sparks
15. Wings of Fire
16. You are Born to Blossom

Websites

1. abdulkalam.com
2. abdulkalam.nic.in
3. brainyquote.com
4. famousquotes.com

5. finestquotes.com
6. freeindia.org
7. iisc.ernet.in
8. indiavision2020.org
9. poetseers.org
10. presidentofindia.nic.in
11. quotationpage.com
12. wikipedia.org
13. wikiquote.org
14. worldofquotes.com

❑